101
Ways to Improve Your
Grammar Skills

101
Ways to
Improve Your
Grammar
Skills

Kris Hirschmann

illustrated by Barbara Levy

*To Gordon, who taught me the correct usage of
"nauseous" and many other things about grammar.
—K.H.*

ISBN 0-8167-7446-3

Printed in Canada.

10 9 8 7 6 5 4 3 2 1

CONTENTS

101

Ways to
Improve Your

Grammar
Skills

Introduction

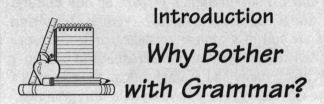

Why Bother with Grammar?

Let's start with the good news. Although you may not realize it, you (yes, *you!*) already know almost everything there is to know about English grammar.

"Now hold on just a minute," you might be thinking. "That's not true at all. I don't know anything about grammar! That's why I bought this book."

Okay, so you might not be able to explain the rules of grammar. But the fact is, *you know most of them.* You have been absorbing grammar since the day you were born. Babies learn to use language by listening to other people talk. By the time you were about three years old, you could probably talk well enough to communicate just about anything you wanted, which means you had a good grasp of grammar. To put it another way: If other people understand you when you speak, you have mastered the basics of English grammar.

That's the good news. Unfortunately, there is also bad news: *English is very complicated.* It includes far more words than any other language. It is also full of exceptions, contradictions, inconsistencies, and shades of meaning.

Because English is so difficult, poor usage is common. People constantly make grammatical mistakes when speaking and writing. And the problem goes beyond everyday folks. Poor grammar is part of our culture! Popular songs contain language errors, television programs are full of grammar mistakes, and newspaper articles often contain written blunders that slip past busy editors. With so many bad examples floating around, it's easy to see why many people have trouble with grammar.

You might wonder why it's important to learn good grammar if so many people are wrong so often. After all, you can understand the essence of what they're saying. Who cares if they make a mistake now and then, right? *Wrong!* Good written and spoken grammar are extremely important. Here are just a few reasons why this is so.

- **Good grammar helps you to communicate.** Sure, you can get your ideas across even if your grammar is poor. But good grammar helps you to say exactly what you mean, so you don't have to worry about being misunderstood. This is especially important when you write. Grammatical errors in writing can confuse your readers. Consistent errors can also frustrate readers and make them give up on whatever you wrote. And hey, if you took the time to write something, you want people to finish reading it!

- **Good written grammar will help your grades.** You're going to have to do a lot of writing throughout your school years, in all sorts of subjects—and no matter what class you are taking, grammar matters. Your science teacher might not grade you specifically on your grammar, but he or she will probably give you a lower mark for a poorly written answer on a test. It goes back to the "communication" thing. If you can't explain yourself well in writing, you cannot expect to be a top student.

- **Your grammar makes an impression.** It may not be fair, but people who use poor grammar when speaking and writing are often thought of as uneducated. The way you present yourself affects the people you will know and the opportunities you will have in life, so it is in your best interest to make sure your grammar is up to par.

So are you ready to work on your grammar skills? If so, great! You're in the right place. This book will help you to fine-tune your speaking and writing by explaining some basic grammatical concepts and some common grammar traps. In all, this book includes 101 hot tips that touch on everything from sentence structure to sound-alike words, from punctuation to general grammatical no-no's. Exercises throughout the book let you practice the concepts as you go. (Answers to the exercises begin on page 99.)

As you read, just remember one thing: You're already an expert. You did all the really hard work when you were a baby. With just a little effort, your grammar skills are sure to shine!

Chapter 1
General Grammar Tips

Are you eager to plunge right into the nitty-gritty of grammatical rules? That's great—but let's hold off for a few pages. There are some general guidelines we need to address first. Why? Because good grammar doesn't start with the actual rules of grammar. It really starts with some fundamental tools and learning techniques.

This chapter will teach you some of these basics. By using your learning skills and by studying the eleven tips on the next few pages, you will create a solid foundation for the more technical grammar work that comes later.

1. Get a good dictionary. A good dictionary provides some important grammar basics. For one thing, it tells you each word's part of speech (noun, verb, adjective, etc.). It also lists the past tenses of verbs—a helpful function since some verbs have more than one past tense form, and some forms are considered more "correct" than others. English usage examples are another handy reference. Many dictionaries show you how a word might be used in everyday speech, and some even provide the usage histories of especially tricky words.

A dictionary can also be a big help when you are trying to figure out which "sound-alike" word to use in a certain situation. A quick glance at the dictionary will tell you, for instance, that a "pear" is a fruit and a "pair" is two of a kind. After reading the definitions of these two words, you are unlikely to confuse them when you write.

2. **Use your computer's grammar checker.** Most computer word-processing programs have built-in grammar-checking software. Grammar checkers are great because they do not just tell you that something is wrong. They also tell you *what* is wrong, and then give you suggestions for fixing it. Running a grammar check on a finished paper or e-mail can help you to catch lots of little mistakes.

One word of caution: Don't depend *too* much on the grammar checker. It will catch lots of errors, but it won't find them all. A grammar checker is just one weapon in your battle for good grammar.

3. **Get your friends' help.** Your friends can be a part of your plan to improve both your spoken and written grammar.

One of the easiest ways your friends can help you is by (kindly) pointing out errors in your speech. Maybe you say "ain't" all the time and you want to break the habit. Or maybe you just can't remember how to use "lie" and "lay" correctly. A friend who has a good grasp of these concepts can tell you when you slip. With time and practice, the right usage will become easier and easier.

Your friends can also help you with your written grammar (and you can help them, too). Read each other's written assignments before handing them in. Your friends may find errors in your writing—and you'll probably see some mistakes that *they* made, too.

4. **Do a lot of reading.** Reading is one of the best ways to expose yourself to correct grammar. The more you read, the more familiar you will become with good English usage, and your grammar will improve. Best of all, this knowledge will be automatic! Things will simply sound "right" or "wrong" to you. You might not know exactly *why* something is right or wrong, but that doesn't really matter. You will *know*.

5. **Pick a "power seat."** Studies have shown that students learn more in certain areas of the classroom. Students who choose seats near the front and middle of the room tend to get the best grades, while those who choose seats near the rear and sides of the room usually do worst.

There's nothing magic about this idea. It boils down to this simple concept: If you are closer to the teacher, it will be easier for you to pay attention. This is partly because you can hear and see the lesson better. It's also because you will not be bothered by the kids who want to pass notes and whisper during class. (It's no surprise that these kids usually sit as far from the teacher as possible!) With fewer distractions, you are much more likely to hear and understand what your teacher has to say.

6. **Get your teacher's help.** If you are stuck on a particular concept, don't hesitate to set up a one-on-one appointment with your teacher. He or she will be glad to give you the individual help you need.

Some students hesitate to admit they are having trouble because they are afraid that it will make them look stupid.

But nothing could be further from the truth. Asking for help proves that you are serious about your studies and therefore makes you look *smarter,* not stupid. It's a can't-lose situation!

7. **Keep a grammar notebook.** If you're like most people, there are a few specific grammar rules that always give you trouble. No matter what you do, you just can't seem to get certain things straight in your head. Get a jump on your grammatical problem areas by writing them down in a special notebook that you keep just for that purpose. Make notes about the mistakes you usually make, as well as the correct usage. You could also jot down some examples. Check your grammar notebook after writing a paper to make sure you haven't fallen into any of your usual grammar traps.

8. **Read your writing out loud.** For most people, speaking correctly is easier than writing correctly. Most students make mistakes when they write that they would never make when talking.

Avoiding these mistakes is easy. Just read your writing out loud to yourself. Listen carefully to your words as you read. Grammatical errors that you didn't notice when you were writing will become obvious—and you can correct them before you hand in your paper or send your e-mail.

9. **Practice, practice, practice.** Like anything else, good grammar takes practice. Reading is the easiest way to practice. You can also do exercises to improve your grammar.

You will probably do some grammar exercises in class. But if the classroom exercises don't help you to understand a concept, then find other sources! Bookstores and teachers' supply stores sell grammar workbooks. You might even be able to find some good grammar books at your local library. Pick up whatever resources you need (ask your teacher for some recommendations) and keep trying until you are sure that you really get it.

10. Quiz yourself on-line. There are tons of grammar websites, and many of them have quizzes that you can take. Here are just a few sites that can help you to improve your grammar skills.

Grammar & Writing Interactive Quizzes
ccc.commnet.edu/grammar/quiz_list.htm
Includes 170 on-line grammar quizzes at various ability levels.

Grammar Bytes!
www.chompchomp.com
Includes sections on grammar terms and rules as well as interactive quizzes.

EnglishCLUB.com
www.englishclub.net/homework/index.htm
Includes quizzes on verb tenses and adjectives.

ESL Quiz Center
www.pacificnet.net/~sperling/quiz/#grammar
This site includes 16 easy-to-take grammar quizzes.

11. Rewrite or rephrase to avoid problem areas. Despite all your efforts, you may find that you are still confused about certain rules of grammar. That's okay. Everyone (even teachers and professional writers) has problem areas. Luckily, you can solve most grammatical problems by finding a different way to say something. The trick here, of course, is understanding your grammar pitfalls so you'll know what words, phrases, and constructions to avoid. Know yourself first, and good grammar will follow.

Chapter 2

Some Grammar Basics

Grammar has a language all its own—and before you can begin to polish your grammar skills, you must understand the language. Words and phrases like "part of speech," "noun," "verb," "subject," "predicate," and "dependent clause," to name just a few, will pop up throughout this book. So a quick refresher course in these important concepts is a good place to start.

As you read this chapter and work the exercises, remember that grammar is a big topic. Many concepts cannot be covered in a short book like this one, and even the concepts that *are* covered cannot be discussed in depth. If you want or need more information on any topic addressed in this chapter, refer to a grammar manual or workbook or ask your teacher for help.

12. **Know your nouns.** A noun is a word that names a person, place, thing, or idea. Nouns can be either singular or plural. Here are some examples:

Person	Place	Thing	Idea
Janet	New York	Jacuzzis	liberty
astronauts	seashore	frog	grace

As well as being singular or plural, nouns can also be either concrete or abstract. A concrete noun names something you can touch, taste, see, hear, or smell. *Dog, automobile, odor,* and *leaf* are concrete nouns. An abstract noun names an idea. *Fury, thought, intelligence,* and *beauty* are abstract nouns.

13. **Pronouns are noun substitutes.** Anytime you see a word such as "she," "it," "my," or "their," you're looking at a pronoun in action. Here's an example. This sentence:

Sarah took Bob and Jamil to the store.

could also be written this way:

She took them to the store.

In the second sentence, the pronoun "She" is a substitute for the noun "Sarah," and the pronoun "them" is a substitute for the nouns "Bob" and "Jamil."

14. **A verb expresses an action or a state of being.** Here are some examples:

Action verbs: hit, breathes, think, went
State of being verbs: is, was, am, are

Verbs can be used in several different tenses. "Love," for example, is in the present tense; "loved" is in the past tense; "will love" is in the future tense.

15. Adjectives modify nouns and pronouns.

"Modify" is basically a way of saying that adjectives tell us more about nouns and pronouns. Here are some examples:

A *green* house   (Which house? The *green* one.)
Swiss cheese   (What kind of cheese? *Swiss*.)
An *angry* bear   (What kind of bear? An *angry* one.)
That girl   (Which girl? *That* one.)
A *little* something   (How much of something? A *little*.)

Several adjectives can be used together to modify one noun. You could talk about "the *big bad* wolf" or "the *lazy, hazy, crazy* days of summer."

16. Adverbs modify verbs, adjectives, and other adverbs.

When adverbs modify verbs, they can explain three things: **how, when,** or **where.** Here are some examples:

The dog sat *quietly*.   (**How** did the dog sit? *Quietly*.)
She *finally* arrived.   (**When** did she arrive? *Finally*.)
Leave it *outside*.   (Leave it **where**? *Outside*.)

When adverbs modify adjectives or other adverbs, they explain **how**. In the sentence *The sun is **too** bright,* "too" is an adverb modifying the adjective "bright." How bright is the sun? *Too* bright. In the sentence *He finished the test **incredibly** quickly,* "incredibly" is an adverb modifying the adverb "quickly." How quickly? *Incredibly* quickly.

17. **Prepositions explain time, direction, position, or a relationship.** Here are some examples:

after the party   (What time? *After*.)
toward the east   (Which direction? *Toward*.)
over the moon   (What position? *Over*.)
tea *with* lemon   (What relationship? *With* each other.)

18. **Conjunctions join words, phrases, or parts of a sentence.** Here are some examples:

silver *and* gold
this *or* that
Katie danced, *but* Kyrin slept.
I'll jump *if* you'll jump!
He'll play *when* his brother arrives.
The chef will prepare your eggs *however* you like them.

19. **Interjections show strong feelings.** These words usually come at the beginning of a sentence, but not always. Here are some examples:

Wow! That cow is huge!
Gosh, I hate it when that happens.
Whoopee! We're going to the amusement park!
I would do it differently, but *hey,* it's your call.

An interjection followed by an exclamation point signals a stronger feeling than one followed by a comma.

20. **A complete sentence contains a subject and a predicate.** A *subject* says what the sentence is about. The subject can be a noun, a pronoun, or a group of words that is used as a noun. A *predicate* says what the subject does or is. The predicate includes the verb plus any other words that are not part of the subject.

In the following examples, the subjects are <u>underlined</u> and the predicates are in **boldface**.

<u>Terry</u> **laughed**.
<u>She</u> **fed the cat**.
<u>The boy next door</u> **collects rocks and stamps**.
<u>P.J. and Robin</u> **went to the movies**.
<u>*Tom Sawyer*</u> **is my favorite book**.

21. **Know the difference between a simple subject and a complete subject.** A simple subject is usually just one noun or pronoun. (The simple subject may be more than one word, however, if it is a proper noun.) It names the main thing the sentence is about. A complete subject is the simple subject plus all the words that go with it to form a phrase.

In the following examples, the complete subjects are <u>underlined</u> and the simple subjects are in **boldface**.

<u>The skateboard **park**</u> is closed on Mondays.
<u>The state of **New Mexico**</u> is usually dry and hot.
<u>The tall radio **tower**</u> could be seen for miles.

22. **Know the difference between a simple predicate and a complete predicate.** A simple predicate is a verb that expresses a sentence's main action or state of being. Depending on its tense, the simple predicate may be up to four words long. A complete predicate is the simple predicate plus all the other words that go with it to form a phrase.

In the following examples, the complete predicates are underlined and the simple predicates are in **boldface**.

That slime **looks** disgusting.
The local mall **was filled** with shoppers.
The ink **would have ruined** my clothes.
Tanya **might have been chosen** for the squad.

23. **Get a grip on compound subjects and predicates.** Compound subjects are two or more nouns or pronouns joined by a conjunction. Compound predicates are two or more simple predicates joined by a conjunction.

In the following examples, the compound subjects are underlined and the simple subjects are in **boldface**.

The home **team** and the visiting **team** shook hands after the game.
Boxes, bags, and paint **cans** filled the garage.

In the following examples, the compound predicates are underlined and the simple predicates are in **boldface**.

The baby **yawned, stretched,** and **wrinkled** her nose.
A good show horse **prances** and **tosses** its mane.

24. **Recognize main and subordinate clauses.** A clause is a group of words that has a subject and a predicate. A main clause can stand on its own as a sentence; a subordinate clause cannot.

In the following examples, main clauses are <u>underlined</u> and subordinate clauses are in **boldface**.

> <u>Suki went to the store</u> **because she ran out of milk**.
> **Before he did his homework**, <u>Danny ate dinner</u>.

25. **Be able to recognize a simple sentence.** A simple sentence has just one complete subject and one complete predicate. Simple sentences can be short or long. They can also contain compound subjects and predicates, as long as there is only one of each.

In the following examples, the complete subjects are <u>underlined</u> and the complete predicates are in **boldface**.

> <u>Joe</u> **coughed**.
> <u>My printer</u> **just ran out of paper**.
> <u>The lady who lives down the street from me</u> **is always sticking her nose into my business**.
> <u>Fluffy and Ginger</u> **hissed and arched their backs**.

26. **Be able to recognize a compound sentence.** A compound sentence contains two or more simple sentences that are joined by a comma (or sometimes a semicolon) and a coordinating conjunction. (The most common coordinating conjunctions are *and, but,* and *or*.)

In each of the following examples, the first simple sentence is underlined and the second is in **boldface**. The coordinating conjunction is in *italics*.

Ray loved to go camping, *but* **none of his friends did**.
I could do my homework, *or* **I could watch TV**.
Shay got a strawberry ice cream cone, *and* **I chose vanilla**.

27. Be able to recognize a complex sentence. A complex sentence contains a simple sentence and a dependent clause. A **dependent clause** contains a subject and a predicate, but it cannot stand alone. The dependent clause begins with a subordinating conjunction. Common subordinating conjunctions include *after, because, before, since, unless, when, whenever,* and *while*.

In the following examples, the simple sentences are underlined and the dependent clauses are in **boldface**. The subordinating conjunctions are in ***boldface italics***. (The subordinating conjunction is part of the dependent clause.)

The dog hides ***whenever*** **I want to give her a bath**.
Mike yelled at the soda machine ***after*** **it ate his change**.
Since **you chose the red game piece**, I guess I'll be green.

28. Sentences can be both compound *and* complex. Compound-complex sentences contain two or more simple sentences and at least one dependent clause. The sentence parts are joined by coordinating and subordinating conjunctions.

The sentences from Tip 27 can easily be changed into compound/complex sentences by adding another simple sentence (<u>underlined</u>). Coordinating conjunctions have been added; they are in *italics*.

The dog hides whenever I want to give her a bath, *and* <u>I have to search for her</u>.

<u>Mike has a terrible temper</u>, *so* he yelled at the soda machine after it ate his change.

Since you chose the red game piece, I guess I'll be green, *but* <u>I'm not happy about it</u>.

Practice 1: Noun Hound
Underline the nouns in the following paragraph.

The spacecraft touched down with a thud. The forest was deserted, so no one saw the ship land. After a few minutes, a door in the side of the ship began to open. Light spilled out as the opening became larger and larger. When the doorway was fully open, a figure in a spacesuit appeared. It was an alien creature! "Hello? Can anyone tell me where to find a bathroom?" it said.

Practice 2: Pronoun Pro
Underline the pronouns in the following paragraph.

Reyna knew she shouldn't do it, but she just couldn't help herself. The opportunity was too good; it might never come again. Putting her misgivings aside, Reyna slipped through the open gate. With one mighty jump, she leaped into the untouched snowbank. It was as cold and perfect as Reyna had imagined. She couldn't help worrying a little bit about old Mr. Jones, though. He was going to throw a fit when he saw what she had done to his yard!

Practice 3: Verb Alert

Underline the verbs in the following paragraph.

The park was a beehive of activity on Saturday afternoon. Babies crawled across the grass as their parents watched. Older children pumped their legs back and forth on the swingset as they tried to reach new heights. Behind the playground, a group of teenagers played a fierce game of basketball. They shouted, ran, and shot baskets as the sun beat down on the court.

Practice 4: Which Modifier?

Underline the adjective or adjectives in each sentence. Circle the adverb or adverbs.

1. Raoul tried to finish the whole burger, but he got too full.

2. The fat pig looked amazingly cute in the pink tutu.

3. Harriet often thought her coach was quite funny.

4. The parade was long, and it moved awfully slowly.

5. The slimy worm quickly squirmed across the wooden table.

6. Jonah wanted to go first, but the new kid beat him to it.

7. My little sister likes only well scrambled eggs.

8. The best Halloween parties have very scary pumpkins.

9. I am fully aware that the exam will be extremely hard.

10. That ugly little frog must leave immediately.

Practice 5: Preposition Finder

Finish each sentence by writing a preposition in the blank space.

1. Suzette hung the picture _____ the wall.

2. The best essay was written _____ Riley.

3. The pitcher tossed the ball _____ the batter.

4. Julio and Anna pass notes _____ class.

5. My snake escaped _____ its cage.

6. I like ketchup _____ my French fries.

7. Read the directions _____ you start.

8. Aisha shoved the laundry _____ her bed.

9. The eggs were hidden _____ the house.

10. The tree fell _____ the storm.

Practice 6: Subject Sleuth

Underline the complete subject in each sentence. Circle the simple subject or subjects.

1. Erin, Deanna, and Shereen are best friends.

2. The little red house at the end of the lane looks deserted.

3. Eggs, flour, and a pinch of salt are needed for this recipe.

4. The robber thought the bank was open until 6:00.

5. The lazy lion slowly opened one eye.

6. While riding their bikes, the boys got caught in a storm.

7. It's raining cats and dogs.

8. The second student from the left just raised her hand.

9. The red Honda and the blue Kia raced down the street.

10. This filthy floor needs a good cleaning.

Practice 7: Spot the Predicates

Underline the complete predicate in each sentence. Circle the simple predicate or predicates.

1. Troy couldn't decide between the licorice and the mints.

2. The magic beanstalk grew and grew and grew.

3. The green socks would have been a better choice.

4. Summer came and went in a flash.

5. We gathered tons of garbage at the clean-a-thon.

6. Maggie and Yvonne talked and giggled all night long.

7. Tarik would like to be elected class president.

8. That isn't my favorite type of music.

9. Georgie could hear her stomach growling during class.

10. My mom will help me to clean and cook the fish I caught.

Practice 8: What's Your Type?

Decide whether each sentence is simple, compound, complex, or compound-complex.

1. I asked Lydia to the movies, but she couldn't go.

2. Wherever you go, there you are.

3. Penguins look like they are wearing tiny tuxedoes.

4. Simon and Jim tried to go swimming as soon as the weather got warm, but the pond was still too cold.

5. No matter what he says, don't drink the potion.

6. Sparks flew from the wand's tip.

7. Even though the shot hurt, Betsy didn't cry, and she felt proud of herself afterward.

8. Robert tried to hit the target, but he missed.

9. The meat loaf looks weird, and it smells funny, too.

10. I was only joking.

11. Call me when the party is over, and I'll come pick you up.

12. Brush your teeth before you go to bed.

13. That roof is too steep to climb.

14. Juanita's hair and makeup looked perfect, and her dress was gorgeous.

15. Although I bought the hint book, I still can't beat that computer game.

16. An alligator can run if it needs to, but it usually just lies around.

17. You can spend your whole allowance, or you can save part of it.

18. I can't finish this assignment until I get more information.

19. Andy and Renee are covered with sand.

20. Although the bee landed on me, it didn't sting me, so no harm was done.

Chapter 3
Teachers' Pet Peeves

Everyone has *pet peeves*, which are words or actions that tend to bother you when you hear or see them. Your teachers are no exception. In fact, *every single teacher* has picky preferences about how things should and should not be done. And there are a few specific grammar mistakes that are practically guaranteed to make your teachers shake their heads in despair. This chapter explains ten of these "grammar traps." Some of these are simply wrong. Others are gray areas. But if you want to get the best possible grades, don't use *any* of them (unless your teacher tells you otherwise, of course).

29. **Avoid useless words and phrases.** In spoken English, the two useless expressions that pop up most frequently are "like" and "you know." A third offender is the word "well." Here's a sentence that falls into all three of these grammar traps: "Well, you know, I went to the store but, like, it was closed, so, you know, I went home."

This example might sound extreme, but don't laugh! Some people talk like this all the time without realizing it. Even YOU probably slip up now and then. Make an effort to break this bad grammar habit; your teachers will thank you for it.

It's easier to avoid useless phrases when you are writing, but pointless words can still slip into your written speech if you're not careful. In particular, dump the phrase "Needless to say . . ." and its cousin, "It goes without saying that . . ." If something truly is so obvious that it doesn't need to be said, you don't need these phrases to point it out.

30. Use "a" and "an" correctly.

The article "a" is used before words that start with consonant sounds: *a house, a bird, a scary thought.* The article "an" is used before words that start with vowel sounds: *an artichoke, an easy task, an honor student* (even though "honor" begins with a consonant letter, the "h" is silent. The initial sound is a short "o").

For whatever reason, "an" is not often used incorrectly. Few people would be tempted to say or write "an nap," "an pancake," and so on. The word "a," on the other hand, is quite often misused, both in speech and in writing. The sentences "May I have a apple?" and "Oh! It's a enormous bug!" are just plain wrong—but to some people, they sound like proper speech.

Don't make this mistake. Learn the difference between "a" and "an," then make sure you use these words correctly.

31. Try not to end sentences with prepositions.

Although this is not a hard-and-fast rule, many teachers hate it when you end sentences with prepositions such as "around," "of," "about," etc. There is even a joke sentence that addresses this problem: "A preposition is a bad word to end a sentence with." The sentence is a joke because the word "with," of course, is a preposition!

To avoid this trap, simply rephrase your sentences. These examples:

> *That bull is nothing to be afraid of.*
> *You gave me something to think about.*

could easily be rewritten to read:

> *There is no need to be afraid of that bull.*
> *I will think about what you said.*

32. Don't split infinitives.

An infinitive is the word "to" followed by a verb—*to go, to study,* and so on. Splitting an infinitive means putting a word between "to" and the verb—*to **boldly** go, to **quietly** study*.

There is no actual rule about this practice. In fact, people who study grammar say there's nothing wrong with splitting the occasional infinitive. However, lots of regular folks (including many teachers) believe that it is a mistake to *ever* split an infinitive. So to be on the safe side, don't do it.

(By the way, did you catch the split infinitive in the previous paragraph? If you think it's "to *ever* split," you're right!)

33. Be careful when using double-negative construction.

Double-negative construction means using two negative-meaning words in the same sentence. In some cases, two negatives cancel each other out and make the sentence mean exactly the opposite of what you meant to say:

*I **don't** want **nothing** right now* actually means *I want something right now.*

*The chickens **didn't** eat **none** of that corn* actually means *The chickens ate some of that corn.*

This topic is especially tricky because some double negatives are not wrong. For example, the following perfectly correct sentence contains two negatives:

*I **wouldn't** go if Lori **weren't** going to be there.*

Study, study, study to learn the difference between the correct and incorrect uses of double negatives.

34. Know when it's okay to start sentences with "And," "But," and "Or."

Some people think that it is always wrong to start a sentence with the words "And," "But," and "Or." However, that's not true. There is nothing technically wrong with using these words to start a sentence, and sometimes they make your writing stronger. Consider these examples:

Billy thought he could ride the horse, but before he knew it, he had been thrown from the saddle.

Billy thought he could ride the horse. But before he knew it, he had been thrown from the saddle.

Read the words out loud. The second example sounds much stronger, doesn't it? Ending the first sentence, pausing, and then moving on to the word "But . . ." adds emphasis to the idea that is being communicated.

There is a down side, however. Although using "And," "But," and "Or" to start sentences can be effective, it is also an easy device to overuse. For this reason, many teachers prefer that students avoid this practice altogether. Ask your teacher how he or she feels, then follow that preference.

35. Learn the difference between "like" and "such as." In traditional grammar, "like" means that things are similar in some way, while "such as" means you are giving examples. The following sentences use "like" and "such as" correctly:

Girls like Judy never win in the end. (The writer is talking about girls who are similar to Judy.)
Little dogs such as dachshunds tend to yap. (The writer is using dachshunds as one example of a little dog.)

This is a really picky pet peeve. Some people care very much about the difference between "like" and "such as." Others claim that the English language has changed so much over the years that there is no longer any difference at all. See how your teacher feels about this one.

36. Write mostly in the active voice rather than the passive voice. "Active voice" means that the subject of the sentence performs the action. "Passive voice" means that an action is done to the subject of the sentence. Active writing is much stronger than passive writing, which is why teachers prefer it in most cases.

These passive sentences:

My tulips were destroyed by hopping rabbits.
Ralph's brain was eaten by aliens.

could easily be rewritten in the active voice:

Hopping rabbits destroyed my tulips.
The aliens ate Ralph's brain.

37. Avoid run-on sentences. Run-on sentences occur when a writer does not use the necessary punctuation and/or conjunction to join two independent clauses.

The following run-on sentences:

Billy got sick he stayed home from school.
Let's trade lunches I like yours better.

can be corrected to read:

Billy got sick, so he stayed home from school.
Let's trade lunches; I like yours better.

38. Avoid sentence fragments, too. A sentence fragment is a group of words that is intended to be a sentence but that is missing either the subject or the predicate.

The following "sentence" is missing a subject:

Bounced up and down. (What bounced? We don't know.)

The following "sentence" is missing a predicate:

The tallest tree in the woods. (What did the tree do? We don't know.)

Fix the first fragment by adding a subject (***The ball bounced up and down***). Fix the second fragment by adding a predicate (*The tallest tree in the woods **fell over last night***).

Practice 1: Like vs. Such As
Write "like" or "such as" in each space.

1. It sure looks _____ a gerbil to me.
2. Friends _____ Jennie and Sam are hard to find.
3. Bright colors, _____ pink and yellow, look best on me.
4. Rae wished there were more books _____ *The Hidden Locket*.
5. Wheeled toys _____ rollerblades can be dangerous.

Practice 2: Run-ons and Fragments
Decide whether each example is a run-on, a fragment, or a complete sentence.

1. We'll use a stopwatch to time ourselves.
2. Chicken is okay I like steak better.
3. After the inspector left the house.
4. The big bird with the colorful feathers.
5. I sure wish it would snow.
6. That skinny boy who has freckles.
7. The CD player is skipping maybe it's broken.
8. That tent keeps falling down.
9. Pilots have the best job they get to fly airplanes!
10. Lena left her mittens under the bridge.

Chapter 4

They Sound the Same . . . But They're Not

English is full of words that sound similar or identical, but that mean different things. Only in English can you "stare at the stair," "sail to the sale," "break the brake," or "brush the hare's hair." It can be hard to remember which spelling refers to which meaning. As a result, sound-alike words are often used incorrectly in writing. (In spoken English, of course, sound-alikes are not an issue. Spelling doesn't matter when you talk!)

This chapter includes fourteen sound-alike word groups that tend to give writers fits. Read the definitions, do the exercises, and memorize the helpful hints. You'll be on your way to better written grammar in no time at all!

39. Don't confuse "except" and "accept." In its most common usage, "except" is a preposition. It means with the exception of: *Everyone except Hector went to the circus.* "Accept" is a verb. It means to receive, approve, or believe: *Denise accepted the award. I was accepted to the gifted program. I accept what you're telling me.*

To keep "except" and "accept" straight, remember that "a" is the first letter of the word "action." "Accept," which is a verb and therefore an action word, also starts with "a."

Practice 1:
Fill in the blanks with "except" or "accept."

1. Please _____ my apology.

2. I like all of the fish _____ the blue one.

3. It rained every day _____ Tuesday.

4. I'm sure the squad will _____ Josie.

40. Don't confuse "affect" and "effect." "Affect" is

a verb. It means to influence something: *His hard work will affect his grade in that course.* "Effect" is usually a noun, and it means the result of something: *His hard work will have a good effect on his grade in that course.*

The word "effect" is also sometimes (though not often) used as a verb. As a verb, the word means to make something happen: *That new law will certainly effect change.*

To keep "affect" and "effect" straight, apply the same rule you learned in Tip 39. "Affect" is an action word; "effect" usually isn't.

Practice 2:
Fill in the blanks with "affect" or "effect."

1. Eating before bedtime _____s my sleep.

2. The hunters' presence had quite an _____ on the deer.

3. The moon's pull _____s the earth's tides.

4. The _____ was not what Danny had intended.

41. Don't confuse "capitol" and "capital." A "capitol" is a building where a state's or country's government meets: *The officials gathered in the capitol.*

The noun "capital" has several meanings. A capital may be the city that contains the capitol: *Pierre is the capital of South Dakota.* It can refer to wealth: *She will need a lot of capital to start her own business.* It can mean an uppercase letter: *Always use a capital at the beginning of a sentence.* And finally, it can refer to the main or most famous city in a certain respect: *Philadelphia is sometimes called the cheesesteak capital of the world.*

If you get mixed up, just remember that "capitol" *only* means a government building. For every other usage, "capital" is the correct word.

Practice 3:
Fill in the blanks with "capitol" or "capital."

1. I think that word should start with a _____.
2. On vacation, we toured the _____ building.
3. Sandy got a job raising _____ for investments.
4. Our nation's _____ is Washington, D.C.

42. **Don't confuse the words "compliment" and "complement."** "Compliment" can be a noun or a verb. As a noun, it means a flattering remark: *She always receives lots of compliments when she wears that beautiful dress.* As a verb, it means to give a compliment: *Bryan complimented Carol on her new hairdo.*

"Complement" can also be a noun or a verb. As a noun, it means something that completes or improves something else: *Gravy is the perfect complement to mashed potatoes.* As a verb, it means to complete or to improve: *The players' styles complemented each other nicely.*

It may help to picture the word "complement" as "comple(te)ment."

Practice 4:
Fill in the blanks with "compliment" or "complement."

1. The workbook is a _____ to the textbook.

2. It never hurts to pay someone a _____.

3. More than one hundred pictures _____ the text.

4. I must _____ you on your excellent term paper.

43. **Don't confuse "stationary" and "stationery."** "Stationary" is an adjective. It means staying in one place: *Judy exercised by riding the stationary bicycle.* "Stationery" is a noun. It means writing materials: *Lisa's stationery is covered with pictures of teddy bears.*

To tell the difference between these words, remember that "stationary," which is an adjective, is the word that contains the "a" instead of the "e"—and "a" stands for "adjective."

Practice 5:

Fill in the blanks with "stationary" or "stationery."

1. Luckily, the car was _____ when its tires blew.
2. Celia got a new box of _____ for her birthday.
3. Wait until the carousel is _____ before you get on.
4. We can get some _____ at the office-supply store.

44. Don't confuse "principle" and "principal."

"Principle" is a noun. It means a basic rule or assumption: *He struggled to learn the principles of geometry.* "Principal" can be a noun or an adjective. As a noun, it usually means the leader of a school or business: *The principal gave me detention. The executives wrote a report for the principals.* As an adjective, it means most important: *Lester has the principal role in the play.*

Here's a memory shortcut for you. Remember this phrase: "The princi*pal* is your *pal.*" That takes care of the noun version of the word. As for the rest . . . well, once again, the "a" in "principal" stands for "adjective."

Practice 6:

Fill in the blanks with "principle" or "principal."

1. The _____ sent a memo to all of the teachers.
2. Jesse lives according to strong moral _____s.
3. I can't let it go; it's the _____ of the thing.
4. Tardiness is my _____ failing.

45. **Don't confuse "then" and "than."** "Then" is an adverb. It indicates a time sequence: *Carrie sneezed, then blew her nose.* "Than" is usually a conjunction. It indicates a comparison: *My brother is two years older than I am. That's easier said than done.*

Practice 7:

Fill in the blanks with "then" or "than."

1. That color is more orange _____ red.

2. I'm happier _____ I ever thought I could be.

3. Brush your hair, _____ we'll go.

4. The lion shook its mane, _____ roared loudly.

46. **Don't confuse "further" and "farther."** "Further" can be an adverb or an adjective. As an adverb, it means to a greater degree: *The disobedient child further annoyed her tired mother.* As an adjective, it means additional: *Eddie needed further help.*

"Farther" can also be an adverb or an adjective. As an adverb, it means to a greater distance: *The library is a little farther down this road.* As an adjective, it means more distant: *There are more coconuts on the farther side of the island.*

Remember that in either form, the word "farther" *always* involves measurable distance. If you could use a ruler on something, "farther" is correct. If not, "further" is the word you're looking for.

Practice 8:

Fill in the blanks with "further" or "farther."

1. Don't go _____ than the stop sign.
2. Let's not discuss this _____.
3. The second ball went _____ than the first.
4. That clarinet player needs _____ practice.

47. **Don't confuse "lie" and "lay."** In their verb forms, "lie" and "lay" are two of the most commonly confused words in the English language. So if you have trouble in this area, you are not alone!

The word "lie" has many definitions. Its most often confused one is to rest in a horizontal position: *The cat lies on its cushion.* The word "lay," too, has many definitions, but its most often confused one is to put in position: *Lay your coat on the couch.*

It might help you to remember that "lay" always requires an object. That is, you must always say *what you're laying* for this word to be correct. You can "lay down the law" (lay what? the *law*) but you can't "lay on the bed" (lay what? We don't know). You can, however, "lay a pillow on the bed" (lay what? a *pillow*).

There is no simple solution to this grammar challenge. Practice until you get it right!

Practice 9:

Fill in the blanks with "lie" or "lay."

1. I'm tired; I think I'll _____ down.
2. Don asked Mary to _____ the table.
3. The hen will _____ an egg today.
4. Some snakes like to _____ in the grass.

48. **Don't confuse "sit" and "set."** The difference between "sit" and "set" is very similar to the difference between "lie" and "lay." In its most common definition, "sit" means to rest on the haunches: *The elephant will sit on that little stool.* The most often confused meaning of "set" is to place: *Rosie set the apple on the table.*

"Sit" is not often used in place of "set." "Set," however, is commonly misused. You might hear someone saying, "I think I'll just set here awhile." Wrong!

Here's a hint. Like "lay," "set" requires an object. If the object is missing, you know the word "set" is wrong.

Practice 10:
Fill in the blanks with "sit" or "set."

1. Let's _____ in the shade and cool off.

2. Andrea _____ the trinket on her windowsill.

3. _____ down; the show is about to start.

4. _____ an extra place for our dinner guest.

49. **Don't confuse "it's" and its.** A lot of people make this mistake, but it's actually an easy one to avoid if you remember that "it's" is *always* a contraction for either "it is" or "it has." In every other circumstance, "its" is correct.

> Right: *It's a bad idea.*
> Right: *The bird carries worms to its babies.*

When in doubt, substitute the words "it is" for "its" or "it's." *It is a bad idea* sounds right, so you know the contraction "it's" is appropriate. *The bird carries worms to it is babies,* however, is obviously wrong, so you must go with "its."

Practice 11:

Fill in the blanks with "it's" or "its."

1. The dirty dog scratched _____ head.

2. _____ going to be stormy tomorrow.

3. I think _____ a shame that this had to happen.

4. That old toy has lost _____ appeal.

50. **Don't confuse "you're" and "your."** These words, too, are easy to tell apart if you remember that "you're" is always a contraction for "you are." In most other circumstances, "your" is correct. (There is another sound-alike word, "yore," which means long ago. But most people don't use this word too much. "You're" and "your" are much more common.)

In these examples, "you're" and "your" are used correctly:

You're my best friend.
Can I borrow your book?

Use the same substitution trick you learned in Tip 49 if you are not sure which word to use. You'll see very quickly that *You are my best friend* is correct, while *Can I borrow you are book?* is not correct.

Practice 12:

Fill in the blanks with "you're" or "your."

1. I wish I had _____ hair!

2. _____ brother invited me to his birthday party.

3. _____ going to love the new roller coaster.

4. While _____ up, please get me some water.

51. Don't confuse "they're," "there," and "their."

Once again, contractions can help you. Start by remembering that "they're" is always a contraction for "they are": *They're going to spend the day at the beach.*

The next two are a little trickier, but still not too tough. "There" is usually an adverb, and it indicates a place or position: *Stand over there. There he is.* "Their" is an adjective, and it indicates possession: *The rock pile blocked their path.* (Whose path? *Theirs*.)

Here's a memory trick to help you. "There" is spelled like "where." If you can ask the question "where" about a sentence (Stand *where*? There. He is *where*? There.), then sound-alike word "there" is the right choice.

Practice 13:

Fill in the blanks with "they're," "there," or "there."

1. _____ standing over _____.

2. _____ shifty eyes gave them away.

3. I don't know why _____ here.

4. _____ are two parts to _____ report.

52. **Don't confuse "too," "two," and "to."** "Too" is an adverb. It can mean either in addition: *Give me some cookies, too!* or overly: *There are too many mosquitoes out tonight.*

"Two" is usually an adjective, and it indicates a number: *Take two aspirin and call me in the morning.*

"To" is usually a preposition. In its most common usage, it indicates movement toward a person, place, or thing: *I biked to school. I gave the gum to Pete.*

For most people, the word "two" isn't the problem. "To" and "too," however, are often confused. Unfortunately, there is no easy trick to remembering how these words are used. This is one more area where practice makes perfect.

Practice 14:
Fill in the blanks with "too," "two," or "to."

1. _____ girls went _____ the zoo.

2. It's _____ rainy _____ play outside.

3. I want a hug, _____.

4. The exam starts in _____ hours.

Chapter 5

Punctuation Blues

Proper punctuation is super simple when you speak. Why? Because there *is* no punctuation in speech—or at least nothing formal. You do use your voice to add question marks, comma pauses, and other verbal punctuation to spoken sentences. But speech punctuation comes much more naturally to most people than the written variety. When you write, there is much more to remember, which means there is much more to get wrong. And unfortunately, punctuation is important. At best, punctuation errors make things hard to read. At worst, they can change the entire meaning of a sentence.

This chapter includes eleven tips that will help you to brush up on your skills and shed those punctuation blues for good!

53. Use the correct punctuation mark to end a sentence.

A sentence can end with one of three punctuation marks: a question mark, an exclamation point, or a period. It is important to use the best one for each sentence.

Question marks end sentences that directly ask for information: *Why did you do that? What is your name?* They should never be used to end sentences that ask indirect questions: *I wonder why the sky is blue. My mom asked me if I had finished my homework.*

Exclamation points end sentences that communicate strong feelings or a sense of urgency: *Look out for that flying brick! I can't take it anymore!* Avoid using too many exclamation points. Save them for when you really need them. And *never* use more than one exclamation point at the end of a sentence!!!!! (like that!)

Any sentence that does not end in a question mark or an exclamation point gets a period.

54. Use commas to separate items in a series.

A series is three or more words or phrases that go together:

hook, line, and sinker
north, south, east, and west
swing the bat, hit the ball, and run to first base

Some writers skip the last comma (which is sometimes called the serial comma). A newspaper reporter, for example, might write *ball, bat and glove*. This structure is not technically wrong. In most types of writing, however, the serial comma is better. Always use it unless a teacher tells you otherwise.

55. Never put a comma between the subject and the predicate.
Some people get into this bad habit and might write: *The car, is making a lot of noise.* Or perhaps: *The car that belongs to Jim, is making a lot of noise.*

It's okay to use a comma after the subject if it is part of a pair surrounding a clause. *The car, which belongs to Jim, is making a lot of noise* is correct. A single comma after the subject, however, always means grammar trouble.

56. Use commas to set off nonrestrictive words or clauses.
This is an important rule. Before we talk about the commas, however, it is important to understand the difference between restrictive and nonrestrictive words and clauses.

A restrictive word or clause is one that is important to the meaning of a sentence. If you took out the word or clause, the meaning of the sentence would change. In these examples:

The dog that belongs to Ralph has fleas.
I'm looking for the book that has a yellow cover.

the underlined clauses cannot be removed without changing the meaning of the sentences. Without those clauses, the reader does not know *which* dog or *which* book the writer is talking about. So they are restrictive clauses.

In these examples, however:

Jeanette's baby, <u>a girl</u>, was born on Thursday.
Snowflakes, <u>which are tiny ice crystals</u>, floated to the ground.

the underlined clauses provide additional information, but they can be removed and the basic point of each sentence does not change. The sentences *Jeanette's baby was born on Thursday* and *Snowflakes floated to the ground* mean essentially the same thing they did before. Therefore, the underlined words are nonrestrictive clauses.

Nonrestrictive clauses are framed by commas, as in the above examples. Restrictive clauses are not.

57. You can also use parentheses to set off nonrestrictive words or clauses. The examples in Tip 56 could be written this way:

Jeanette's baby (a girl) was born on Thursday.
Snowflakes (which are tiny ice crystals) floated to the ground.

Parentheses tend to make the enclosed information seem more "separate" from the rest of the sentence than commas do. Use parentheses if you want to strengthen the extra-information feeling of a nonrestrictive clause. If you want your nonrestrictive clause to flow smoothly with the rest of the sentence, however, then commas are the way to go.

58. Know how to use a semicolon correctly.
Semicolons join two independent clauses into one sentence:

Mae isn't my mother; she's my aunt.
We're running late; let's get going!

Semicolons can also be used to separate items in a series if the items themselves already contain commas:

My parents met with Ms. Kaplan, the principal; Mr. Gonzalez, the vice principal; and Ms. Smith, the guidance counselor.

59. Know how to use a colon correctly.
Colons have several uses. They may introduce examples. (If you look carefully, you will see that colons are used for this purpose throughout this book.) Colons may also introduce lists:

Raoul has three sisters: Miriam, Ramona, and Felice.

or quoted material:

In her speech, the congresswoman declared: "It is time to pay attention to the needs of the masses."

Colons are also used after greetings in letter writing:

To whom it may concern:

and between the hour and the minutes in expressions of time:

3:25 a.m.

Never use a colon if the sentence would make sense without it. The colon in the sentence *The Easter basket contained: candy, toys, and dyed eggs* is wrong even though it introduces a list. The sentence reads just fine without the extra punctuation, so it should be left out.

60. Put apostrophes in the correct place when forming contractions.

A contraction is two words squeezed into one. In a contraction, one or more letters are dropped and replaced with an apostrophe. Here are some examples:

I am	I'm
You will	You'll
It would	It'd
Who is	Who's
Do not	Don't

The most common contraction error happens with "not" contractions such as *had not/hadn't, did not/didn't,* and so on. It is not unusual for people to place the apostrophe before the "n": *had'nt, did'nt, do'nt.* But this is wrong. The apostrophe always goes between the "n" and the "t." Just remember that in a contraction, the apostrophe takes the place of any missing letters. In "not" contractions, it takes the place of the "o." So you know where that punctuation has to go!

61. Put apostrophes in the correct place when forming possessives.

To make a singular noun possessive, add *'s* to the end:

Darla's necklace
the car's muffler
Paris's sights

To make a plural noun that ends in "s" possessive, add a single apostrophe to the end:

the boats' wakes
the teachers' lounge

To make a plural noun that does not end in "s" possessive, add *'s* to the end:

the sheep's bleats
the men's room

Remember that these rules do not apply to pronouns. Most pronouns take entirely different forms when they are possessive. "He" becomes "his," "they" becomes "their," and so on. One of the most common mistakes in the English language—writing "it's" as a possessive form of "it"—happens because people forget that pronouns are not the same as nouns where possession is concerned.

62. **Know the difference between hyphens and dashes.** A hyphen is a short line that joins words. Joined words are called compound words. Here are some examples:

old-fashioned
self-confidence
great-uncle

You may also see a hyphen used to divide a single word when the whole word doesn't fit on one line:

Mary asked her teacher for help, because she didn't understand her homework assignment.

A dash is a long line (sometimes typed as two hyphens in a row). Dashes can sometimes substitute for commas, colons, and parentheses. They separate chunks of information within a sentence. Here are some examples:

He tried to keep his balance—but he fell over anyway.
My favorite shirt—the red one—is in the wash.
Ms. Murrah is a great teacher—she is always willing to help me when I need it.

Hyphens should never be used in place of dashes. If you are trying to separate ideas, remember that you need a *long* line! Check with your teacher about dash usage, however. Dashes have so many functions that they are easy to overuse. Also, they tend to give writing a more casual flavor. For these reasons, some teachers prefer that you avoid dashes altogether.

63. **Know when to use an ellipsis.** An ellipsis is written as three dots with spaces in between (. . .). It is usually used to show that some words have been left out of a quotation. This phrase, for example:

Jonas went to work one fine morning (even though he would have preferred to stay at home), only to discover that his office had burned down during the night.

could be written like this:

Jonas went to work one fine morning . . . only to discover that his office had burned down during the night.

The writer of the second version gets the best of both worlds. She gets a shorter sentence, and she also gets credit for accuracy because her ellipsis shows clearly that something was deleted from the original text.

An ellipsis can also be used to end a sentence that trails off without a true ending:

"Why did you leave the neighborhood without permission?" demanded Ahmad's father.
"Well, I, uh . . ." Ahmad stuttered.

Like dashes, ellipses are good for effect but are easy to overuse. To improve your writing, use ellipses only when absolutely necessary.

Practice 1: End the Sentence
Put the best punctuation mark at the end of each sentence.

1. What is the new girl's name ___

2. I'm so excited I could just shriek ___

3. Get over here right this second ___

4. Bears hibernate in the winter ___

5. Where did you get that sweater ___

6. Water the plants twice a week ___

7. I can't believe he said that ___

8. Who do you think will win the election ___

9. The garbage is collected on Fridays ___

10. Our team is about to win the game ___

Practice 2: Colon or Semicolon?
Fill in the blanks with the correct punctuation.

1. Their pets included Bobby, a bunny ___ Steven, a dog ___ and Philip, a cockatiel.

2. Meet me on the playground at 5___15.

3. I painted the room in my favorite colors ___ green, blue, and yellow.

4. That toast is ruined ___ throw it out.

5. U.S. patriot Patrick Henry once said ___ "Give me liberty or give me death."

6. Dear Sirs ___ Please cancel my subscription.

7. Selma had a problem ___ She could never sleep the night before a test.

8. This uniform is too dirty to wear ___ besides, it's too small.

Practice 3: Word Squeeze
Turn the underlined words into contractions.

1. It has been a long time since dinosaurs were alive.

2. They are going to love this gift.

3. I wish it did not have to be this way.

4. Here is our turnoff.

5. The tiger would not jump through the hoop.

6. Raisins were not Zev's favorite fruit.

7. We have had six substitute teachers this year.

8. Maybe it will rain tomorrow.

9. Who is knocking at the door?

10. We are going to play a game tonight.

Practice 4: Get Possessive

Add apostrophes to the underlined words to make them possessive.

1. The school newsletter published <u>Robins</u> poem.

2. Paige was amazed by the <u>leaves</u> colors.

3. The <u>calves</u> muzzles were white with milk.

4. The <u>parrots</u> feathers were mostly green.

5. Can I go study at <u>Eds</u> house?

6. The <u>womens</u> room needs a good cleaning.

7. I waved to the <u>oxens</u> owner.

8. That <u>phones</u> shrill ring is incredibly annoying.

9. The <u>hamsters</u> cages are starting to stink.

10. My cat will guard the <u>mices</u> holes.

Chapter 6
Commonly Misused Words and Phrases

Many of the most common mistakes in English involve easily confused words or phrases. Even though some of these words and phrases sound nothing alike, they are used incorrectly all the time, both in speech and in writing.

This chapter explains ten of the most frequently misused words and phrases in the English language. Many of these are misused so often, in fact, that few people can tell the difference between correct and incorrect usage. But *some* people can—and you're about to become one of them!

64. **Don't misuse "that" and "which."** The words "that" and "which" have many uses. The one that causes the most confusion is the use of "that" and "which" as pronouns to introduce restrictive and nonrestrictive clauses. (See pages 55 and 56 for a discussion of restrictive and nonrestrictive clauses.)

When choosing between "that" and "which," always start a restrictive clause with "that." In the following examples, the restrictive clauses are <u>underlined</u>:

Birds <u>that fly north in the spring</u> have strong wings.
I'm listening to the CD <u>that you lent me</u>.

Again assuming that you are choosing between "that" and "which," always start a nonrestrictive clause with "which." In the following examples, the nonrestrictive clauses are <u>underlined</u>:

Curry, <u>which is an Indian dish,</u> is too spicy for me.
It took ages to reach the clinic, <u>which was miles away.</u>

65. **Don't misuse "who" and "that."** "Who" is used to introduce clauses that refer to people or animals with names. "That" is used to introduce clauses that refer to anything else, including unnamed animals.

Right:

*My sister, **who** had just taken a bath, was fresh and clean.*
*His pride was the only thing **that** got hurt in the tumble.*

Wrong:

*The boy **that** lives next door has blond hair.*
*Let's feed the stray cat **who** keeps coming to our door.*

66. Don't misuse "who" and "whom." "Who" is a subject pronoun. In other words, it does something:

That is the boy who pulled my hair. (In this sentence, "who" refers to the boy who *did* the pulling.)

"Whom" is an object pronoun. In other words, something is done to it:

That is the boy to whom I lent my book. (In this sentence, "whom" refers to the boy who *was lent* something.)

The difference between "who" and "whom" is tough for lots of people. The easiest way to figure out the difference is to substitute the pronouns "he" and "him" for "who" or "whom." If "he" sounds right (*He pulled my hair*), then "who" is the correct word. If "him" sounds right (*To him I lent my book* or, rearranged, *I lent my book to him*), then "whom" is the word you need.

67. Don't misuse "can" and "may." Use "can" when you want to express an ability:

Luisa is smart; she can pass the test.
That kangaroo sure can jump.

Use "may" when you want to express permission or uncertainty:

You may leave the table when you finish eating.
The bridge may collapse if it isn't repaired.

68. **Don't misuse "good" and "well."** Many people mistakenly use the adjective "good" in place of the adverb "well."

In the following examples, "good" is meant to modify verbs. But adjectives do not modify verbs, so "good" is the wrong choice in these cases:

Our team did good in the playoffs.
My new scooter runs good!

To correct these sentences, substitute "well" for "good":

Our team did well in the playoffs.
My new scooter runs well.

Usage Note: In spoken English, the incorrect use of the word "good" is extremely common. Even people who know better often use "good" as an adverb in casual speech. Because this spoken "error" is accepted by all but the pickiest grammarians, it is more important to be careful about your usage of "good" and "well" when writing than when speaking.

69. **Don't misuse "real" and "really."** The difference between "real" and "really" is similar to the difference between "good" and "well." "Real" is an adjective; "really" is an adverb. These sentences:

The sun is shining real bright today.
Although Miko pedaled real fast, she couldn't keep up.

should be corrected to read:

The sun is really bright today.
Although Miko pedaled really fast, she couldn't keep up.

70. Don't misuse "smell" and "stink."

There is a fine distinction between the verb forms of these two words. Some grammarians, in fact, say that there is no difference. But careful writers use "smell" when the action has an object, and "stink" when it does not.

Right:

Can you smell the lilacs? (Smell what? The lilacs.)
Whatever you're cooking, it smells great. (Smells how? Great.)
That skunk sure does stink. (There is no object.)

Wrong:

Take the garbage out; it smells. (Smells what? Smells how? We don't know because there is no object.)

71. Don't misuse "fewer" and "less."

People often use the word "less" when they really mean "fewer." "Fewer" refers to anything that can be counted. "Less" refers to things that cannot be counted. The following sentences:

Sondra has less jelly beans than David does.
That tree has less leaves than it did a month ago.

should be corrected to read:

Sondra has fewer jelly beans than David does.
That tree has fewer leaves than it did a month ago.

Jelly beans and leaves can be counted, so "fewer" is the correct word in these cases.

On the other hand, these sentences:

Sondra has less freedom than David does.
The tree is less beautiful than it was a month ago.

are correct, because freedom and beauty cannot be counted.

72. **Don't misuse "*i.e.*" and "*e.g.*"** The abbreviation "*i.e.*" stands for *id est*, which means "that is" in Latin. It is used to introduce a clarification:

All of those blouses look the same, i.e., *they are all pink with purple buttons.*

The abbreviation "*e.g.*" stands for *exempli gratia*, which means "for example" in Latin. As the translation suggests, "*e.g.*" is used to introduce examples:

Long-haired dogs, e.g., *huskies and St. Bernards, are uncomfortable in hot weather.*

To avoid confusion, it is usually better to write "that is" or "in other words" instead of "*i.e.*," and "for example" instead of "*e.g.*"

73. Don't misuse "different than" and "different from."

There is only one situation in which "different than" is acceptable: when it precedes a descriptive clause. The following examples are correct:

The parade is different than it was last year.
The clouds look different than they did a minute ago.

In all other cases, use "different from":

A soccer ball is different from a volleyball.
Knowledge is different from wisdom.

74. Be careful with the phrase "I could care less."

Lots of people use this phrase when they really mean to say "I *couldn't* care less." The sentence *I could care less about what Pasha thinks* means exactly what it says upon careful reading. The writer *could care less,* which means he or she cares at least a little bit already. The sentence is correct, but chances are it doesn't express what the writer actually meant.

Use "I couldn't care less" if that's what you really mean. Or better yet, just say "I don't care." It means the same thing and it's not as awkward.

Practice 1: Finish the Sentences

In each sentence, two words appear in parentheses. Underline the correct word.

1. Rover was the only dog (that, who) refused to eat.

2. I like rides (that, who) turn upside down.

3. Becky met a boy (that, who) likes to ski.

4. The movie (that, which) we saw last night was boring.

5. Chen opened the gate, (that, which) was old and rusty.

6. Ben stayed home, (that, which) was unusual.

7. The boy (who, whom) the teacher scolds every day is going to end up suspended.

8. Leila especially liked the clown (who, whom) blew bubbles.

9. The coach (who, whom) Cory likes is standing by the referee.

10. The robot (can, may) speak four languages.

11. I (can, may) go to the game if I'm not busy.

12. (Can, May) your dog catch a Frisbee?

13. It is important to speak and write (good, well).

14. I gave the car a (good, well), thorough cleaning.

15. Are you feeling (good, well) today?

16. Franz is (real, really) good at algebra.

17. In the movie, the puppet turns into a (real, really) boy.

18. Jessica (real, really) likes Tyler.

19. I think I (smell, stink) a rat.

20. This experiment might make the lab (smell, stink).

21. Sam could (smell, stink) Aunt Betty's perfume long after she had gone.

22. Give the horses (fewer, less) water next time.

23. It would be nicer here if there were (fewer, less) bugs.

24. Jamie has (fewer, less) freckles than Sarah.

25. Peter raises reptiles, (*e.g.*, *i.e.*) snakes and geckos.

26. She had to attend a "Saturday study hall," (*e.g.*, *i.e.*) detention.

27. Marissa reads all types of books, (*e.g.*, *i.e.*) mysteries and biographies.

28. Your answer is different (from, than) mine.

29. My teacher looks different (from, than) he did yesterday.

30. That skateboard is different (from, than) this one.

31. He doesn't care much, but I suppose he (could, couldn't) care less.

32. I can't stand this song, and I (could, couldn't) care less if I never hear it again.

33. Jordan thinks Kasey is mean, and she (could, couldn't) care less if Kasey never spoke to her again.

Chapter 7

I Couldn't Agree More

In most areas of life, agreement is just nice. In language, however, it's essential. Good grammar depends on agreement between verb tenses, singular and plural word forms, subjects and verbs, sentence structure, and much more.

This chapter discusses eight common agreement mistakes. It also includes several exercises that will let you practice your grammar skills. You can read up, then test yourself to make sure you've really got it!

75. Make sure your verb tenses agree. Within a sentence, verb tenses must agree with each other. In the following examples, the verb tenses do not agree:

I slept while Billy drives. ("slept" is past tense, but "drives" is present tense)

The grill smokes when we cooked the hamburgers. ("smokes" is present tense, but "cooked" is past tense)

These sentences can be corrected to read:

I sleep while Billy drives or *I slept while Billy drove.*
The grill smokes when we cook the hamburgers or
The grill smoked when we cooked the hamburgers.

It is pretty easy to see that the first two examples are wrong. Tense agreement gets a little harder, however, when you get into the present perfect, past perfect, and future perfect. Take this example:

I will have returned from the store by the time you finished your homework.

Once again the verb tenses do not agree. "Will have returned" is in the future perfect tense; "finished" is in the past tense. To make this sentence correct, "finished" should be changed to "have finished" (present perfect) or "finish" (present). The sentence will mean something slightly different depending on which tense you choose, but both choices are right.

76. Match singular subjects with singular verbs and plural subjects with plural verbs. This rule is a no-brainer most of the time. Things can get confusing, however, when a singular subject is modified by a plural prepositional or adverbial phrase, or vice versa. It can be very tempting to match the verb to the modifying phrase rather than to the subject, as in these examples:

*The cat with the seven kittens were playing in the sun.
The chairs, along with the table, was sitting on the porch.*

Both examples are grammatically incorrect. The subject of the first sentence is the singular noun "cat," so the verb must be singular as well:

The cat with the seven kittens was playing in the sun.

The subject of the second sentence is the plural noun "chairs," so the verb must be plural as well:

The chairs, along with the table, were sitting on the porch.

Pay attention to your singular/plural construction to avoid making mistakes like these.

77. Match singular indefinite pronouns with singular verbs and plural indefinite pronouns with plural verbs.

Indefinite pronouns stand for nouns in a very general way. The indefinite pronoun "everybody," for example, stands for an entire group of people without singling out any one person.

A few indefinite pronouns, including "both," "few," "many," "others," and "several," are always plural. These pronouns need plural verbs:

Many go to the beach on Labor Day.
Several were found at the bottom of the pool.

Most indefinite pronouns, however, are singular. That includes seemingly plural pronouns such as "everyone," "anybody," and "everything." These pronouns need singular verbs:

Everyone knows the answer to that question.
Anybody has the right to a good education.

A few indefinite pronouns, including "all," "any," "most," "none," and "some," can be singular or plural depending on the usage:

Most of those cats bite. (several cats out of a group, so more than one; therefore, use the plural verb "bite")

Most of the ride was boring. (part of a single ride, so less than one; therefore, use the single verb "was")

When deciding which verbs to use with indefinite pronouns, be particularly careful with the singular pronouns. Because they seem like they should be plural, they tend to cause the most confusion.

78. Match collective nouns with singular or plural verbs depending on the situation.

Collective nouns refer to groups of people, things, or animals. "Club," "bunch," and "herd" are examples of collective nouns.

Collective nouns can be either singular or plural. They are singular if the group is acting as a unit:

The club goes to one play each month.
The flower bunch was tied with a red ribbon.
The herd traveled slowly across the prairie.

The very same nouns are plural, however, if the different members or parts of the group are acting separately:

The club argued about their membership fees.
Some of the bunch were wilting.
The herd were led into individual pens.

Read carefully to see whether a group is acting together or separately, then make your verbs singular or plural to match.

79. Be extra careful with the plural pronouns "they" and "their."

Lazy writers often use the pronoun "they" when they really mean "he or she," and "their" when they really mean "his or her." Consider these examples:

A person must sometimes do things they don't like.
Each player throws their dice.

In these examples, the writer is probably trying to avoid these correct but wordier sentences: *A person must sometimes do things he or she doesn't like* and *Each player throws his or her dice*. "Each player" and "A person" are both singular, so they cannot take the plural pronouns "they" and "their."

Don't fall into this trap. Either make your subjects plural to match your pronouns, or use the correct singular pronouns. Or better yet, rewrite the sentences to avoid those irritating pronouns altogether.

80. Match up the two parts of the conjunctions "either . . . or" and "neither . . . nor."

"Either . . . or" and "neither . . . nor" are correlative conjunctions. "Correlative" simply means used together, and that is the key to this rule. When used as a conjunction, "either" is always used with "or" and "neither" is always used with "nor." Here are some examples:

Either you give me the salt or I'll just grab it.
Neither the gorilla nor the zebra likes the zookeeper.

Never use "either" with "nor" or "neither" with "or." (The second mistake, by the way, is more common.)

81. Don't let your modifiers dangle.

A modifier is a clause that provides extra information about the subject of the sentence. Although modifiers can go anywhere, most problems occur when they are placed at the beginning of a sentence. The modifier always refers to the subject—but all too often, careless writers arrange their sentences so the modifier "dangles," or refers to something it shouldn't. Here are some examples:

While grading the papers, three common mistakes were noticed by our teacher. (Who graded the papers? The teacher. But "mistakes" is the subject of this sentence.)
Walking to school, a car almost hit me. (Who walked to school? Me. But "car" is the subject of this sentence.)
Because it is wet, I think the lawn was watered today. (What is wet? The lawn. But "I" is the subject of this sentence.)

These sentences could be rewritten to read:

While grading the papers, our teacher noticed three common mistakes.
Walking to school, I was almost hit by a car.
I think the lawn was watered today; it is wet.

For good grammar's sake, make sure modifiers agree with the subject of the sentence.

82. Pay attention to parallel structure.

"Parallel structure" is a fancy way of saying that different parts of a sentence should have the same grammatical construction. "Running," for example, parallels "biking," but not "walk" (which lacks the "ing" ending). "English" parallels "math," but not "playing volleyball" (which contains a verb and therefore is constructed differently).

The following sentences do not follow the parallel structure rule:

My friend Lisa is nice and always helps me.
My hobbies are reading, surfing, and baseball.

These sentences could be corrected to read:

My friend Lisa is nice and helpful.
My hobbies are reading, surfing, and playing baseball.

Keeping an eye on parallel structure is an easy way to make sure your writing agrees. Follow this rule and you'll be on your way to better grammar in no time at all!

Practice 1: Verb Choice

In each sentence, two words appear in parentheses. Underline the correct word.

1. The leaves fell when the wind (blew, blows).

2. The rhino (snorts, snorted) and shakes its horn.

3. I would study if I (had, would have) the right books.

4. Trey (has eaten, ate) at that restaurant before he came over.

5. The waves crashed as the tide (rolls, rolled) in.

6. Some pages of the book (was, were) bent at the corners.

7. The people on the roller coaster (looks, look) sick.

8. The polish on Suki's toenails (is, are) bright red.

9. Vitamins with calcium (is, are) good for your bones.

10. The picture of the puppies (was, were) my favorite.

11. Everybody (think, thinks) I look like my sister.

12. Some of the universe (have been, has been) explored.

13. Each has (their, its) own purpose.

14. Anything on this table (cost, costs) one dollar.

15. I believe in magic, but others (does, do) not.

16. The family (goes, go) on vacation every year.

17. The litter (scramble, scrambles) all over the bed.

18. This class (meets, meet) three times per week.

19. The class (were, was) arguing with the teacher.

20. The band mostly (play, plays) Top 40 hits.

Practice 2: They and Their

The pronoun "their" appears in the following sentences. Decide whether each sentence is correct or incorrect.

1. A parent should never leave their baby alone.

2. A good dog always obeys their owner.

3. The birds carried sticks to their nest.

4. Every child received their own goodie bag.

5. The players poured ice water on their coach's head.

Practice 3: Spot the Danglers

Each of the following sentences begins with a modifying phrase. Decide whether each phrase is correct or whether it is a "dangler."

1. When dressed for the prom, Angie looked like a princess.
2. To improve your grammar, it would be good to study harder.
3. If properly installed, you should have no trouble with that switch.
4. After swimming in the pond, Aaron noticed that it was full of snakes.
5. Although it was simple, the scientist flubbed the experiment.

Practice 4: Parallel Structure

Each of the following sentences contains structures that may or may not be parallel. Decide whether each sentence is correct or incorrect.

1. The driver slammed on the brakes and was blowing the horn.
2. One, three, five, and seven are all prime numbers.
3. Chen wants to go skating, shopping, and eat ice cream.
4. Put a fork, a knife, and a spoon by each plate.
5. My boss praised me for my hard work and going beyond the call of duty.

Chapter 8

Use with Care
. . . Or Not
At All!

English is full of words and phrases that seem harmless but that can destroy your grammar. Some of these "danger words" are perfectly acceptable when used correctly but just plain wrong when not. Others aren't exactly wrong, but they are imprecise and generally worth avoiding. Still other words and phrases are wrong no matter how or where you use them. And yet many people still do, to the dismay of English teachers everywhere.

This chapter highlights twelve words and phrases to use with extreme care . . . or not at all. When you have finished reading all twelve tips, you will be way ahead in the grammar department. Start paying attention to the things other people say. You will be astonished at how often these errors crop up!

83. Never use "ain't." The word "ain't" started out as a contraction for "am I not." It has been around since the late 1700s and at one time was used by everyone, even the most educated people. Today, however, "ain't" is considered a non-word, and those who use it are seen as uneducated. Don't let people get this impression of you! Avoid using "ain't" in your speech and writing to stay out of this trap.

84. Never use "irregardless." This word is so common in spoken and written English that many people think it's perfectly correct. But it is not!

Here's the problem. The word "regardless" is negative in meaning. The prefix "ir-" is also negative (it basically means "not," as in the word "irrational" = not rational). "Irregardless," then, is a double negative. You could also say that it is redundant (needlessly repetitive).

Instead of "irregardless," simply use "regardless." You will be correct every time, and people who appreciate good grammar will thank you.

85. Never use "overexaggerate." The problem with "overexaggerate" is similar to the problem with "irregardless": The word is redundant. "Exaggerate" means to overstate. By adding the prefix "over-," you end up with a word that means "over overstate." When you look at it that way, it's obvious that the word makes no sense.

The solution is simple. Good old "exaggerate"—*without* the "over"—will communicate what you want to say.

86. Never use "for free." This phrase pops up all too often in both written and spoken English. You have probably heard (and perhaps said or written) things like this:

He gave me the basketball cards for free.
This ticket will get me into the park for free.

Common? Yes. Correct? No! "Free" is an adjective, and prepositions (including "for") do not modify adjectives. They modify nouns or pronouns. So a ticket might get you into the park for *nothing* (a pronoun), or it might simply get you into the park *free*—no "for" about it.

There is only one reason that "for" and "free" might bump into each other, and that is if "free" is sandwiched between "for" and the noun it modifies, as in these sentences:

*She looked **for free stuff** at the convention.*
*I only went there **for free food**.*

If you're using the word "free" on its own, however, the combination "for free" is always a no-no.

87. Never use "could of," "might of," "would of," "should of." All of these phrases are wrong, wrong, wrong! The correct phrases are "could have," "might have," "would have," "should have."

As with so many grammatical errors, this one is more common in written English. The written errors are probably due to the fact that most people contract the correct phrases when they are speaking: "could've," "might've," "would've," "should've." When spoken, "could've" sounds just like "could of," so it is not surprising that many people make this mistake when writing. But *you* don't have to!

88. Never use "try and."
This is another phrase that many people use, but it's always wrong. The correct phrase is "try to."

Wrong: *I'll try and call you later tonight.*
Right: *I'll try to call you later tonight.*

No deep explanation is needed for this one. It's just sloppy English. Don't do it.

89. Be careful with the word "nauseous."
"Nauseous" is a sneaky word because it does not mean what you probably think it does. Lots of people believe that "nauseous" means queasy, as in "I feel nauseous." In traditional English, however, the word actually means causing nausea. So in the pickiest sense, a person who claims to feel nauseous is actually saying that he or she makes other people feel sick to their stomachs. The more correct usage is "I feel nauseated."

The usage of "nauseous" is loosening up. Most grammarians say that "I feel nauseous" and similar usages have become so common that they are now acceptable. However, lots of people still follow the old rules and will think you are wrong if you use "nauseous" in the modern sense. So in the interest of good grammar, it is best to avoid this word as much as possible.

90. Be careful with the word "hopefully."
"Hopefully" is another word that doesn't necessarily mean what you think it does. The word means with hope, as in these examples:

Pen in hand, Ben hopefully approached the sports hero.
The hungry dog sniffed the plate hopefully.

"Hopefully" never means I hope, or it is to be hoped, as in these examples:

Hopefully, I will do well on tomorrow's exam.
Clara fell off her bike, but hopefully she will be all right.

Almost everybody makes this mistake. But that doesn't mean *you* have to do it—especially in writing, where the error is especially noticeable. If you feel inclined to use "hopefully" in this way, rewrite you sentence instead:

I hope I will do well on tomorrow's exam.
Clara fell off her bike, but we're hoping she will be all right.

91. Be careful with the word "literally." "Literally" means actually. When you use the word "literally," you warn the listener or reader that your words mean precisely what they say:

I was literally on my way out the door. (The writer was actually stepping through the door.)
The room was literally lightless. (There was not even a glimmer of light in the room.)

Too many speakers and writers, however, use "literally" to mean virtually or almost, as in these examples:

We were literally dead on our feet. (Not likely if you're still here to talk about the experience.)
I'm so hot, I'm literally on fire. (Quick! Call the fire department!)

Know the meaning of "literally" and use the word only when it is appropriate.

92. Be careful with the word "unique." "Unique" means like no other. Many people, however, use the word "unique" when talking about things that probably aren't all that special:

a unique shopping experience
a unique taste sensation

Save "unique" for when you really need it. Oh, and by the way, *never* use phrases such as "more unique," "most unique," "extremely unique," and so on. "Unique" is already a superlative, which means the word can't get any better or bigger no matter how many modifiers you add.

93. Be careful with the word "unbelievable." "Unbelievable" means not to be believed. Unfortunately, this word is used in lots of situations that actually are quite believable:

He balanced on the pole for fifteen minutes. It was unbelievable. (Come on, now. It isn't *that* unbelievable. After all, the writer saw it happen.)

Jordan's behavior is unbelievable. (The behavior may be unacceptable, but the fact remains that Jordan does behave this way.)

Try not to overuse this word. Save "unbelievable" for when you truly don't believe something (*Nathaniel's lies are unbelievable*), or for when you simply can't think of any other way to emphasize a point you are trying to make.

94. **Do not overuse the words "very" and "really."** These words aren't wrong, but they are weak. "Very tired" can be replaced by "exhausted"; "really pretty" can be replaced by "beautiful." Dump "very" and "really" as often as you can. You will find that your writing and speaking become stronger and more colorful as a result.

Chapter 9
Grab Bag

Congratulations! You have nearly completed your grammatical journey. But before you call it quits, there are just a few more things you should know—and they are all packed into this short final chapter.

The tips on the next few pages do not fit neatly into any category; they're all over the map. That's why this chapter is called "Grab Bag." Reach into the bag and grab whatever you like. No matter what you choose, good grammar is the guaranteed prize!

95. In order to avoid confusion, do not overuse pronouns.
As you already know, pronouns are noun substitutes. When used properly, pronouns make your speech and writing much crisper. *Jim asked Jim's mother if Jim could go to the park,* for example, is awkward. But pronouns clean that sentence right up: *Jim asked his mother if he could go to the park*.

Although pronouns are handy, they can also be overused. Consider this sentence:

Ralph said he would meet Herb at the library, but he was late, so he got mad at him.

Who was late and who got mad? It's unclear. The problem with this sentence is too many pronouns. Putting some nouns back in will help the writer to communicate what he or she means:

Ralph said he would meet Herb at the library, but Herb was late, so Ralph got mad at him.

96. Know when to use subject and object pronouns. A subject pronoun performs an action:

She wrapped the gift. (**She** does the wrapping.)

An object pronoun receives an action:

I took a picture of her. (A picture was taken of **her**.)

Subject and object pronouns are often confused, especially in compound use: *Greg and I, him and me,* and so on. Someone might write or say, for example:

Sasha and me went to the mall.
The cake was split between she and I.

Both of these sentences are wrong. In the first sentence, "me" is part of a compound subject that is performing an action, so the correct pronoun is "I" (*Sasha and I went to the mall*). In the second sentence, "she and I" both receive the action of splitting the cake, so both pronouns should be in the object form (*The cake was split between her and me*).

There is a good trick for keeping subject and object pronouns straight. When in doubt, mentally skip the other words in the compound phrase and say the rest of the sentence to yourself. *Me went to the mall* is obviously wrong. *The cake was split between she* and *The cake was split between I* both sound wrong, too. By using this technique, you can easily decide which pronouns go where.

97. Be particularly careful with the pronoun "myself."

Some people just love to toss this pronoun into the strangest places:

John and myself are going to grab a bite to eat.
The dog licked myself and my brother.

To some ears, the use of "myself" makes these sentences sound refined. To educated ears, however, they just sound wrong! The sentences should read:

John and I are going to grab a bite to eat.
The dog licked me and my brother.

The trick you learned in Tip 96 applies here, too. Get rid of the extra words in the compound phrase to see whether or not "myself" applies. *Myself (is) going to grab a bite to eat* and *The dog licked myself* sound awful, so you know the usage is wrong.

98. **Avoid redundant phrases.** Some common phrases are redundant and should not be used. Here are some examples:

future plans (Why is it redundant? Because all plans involve the future.)
small in size (Why is it redundant? Because "small" automatically refers to size.)
free gift (Why is it redundant? Because gifts by definition are free.)

These phrases could be shortened to one word each: *plans*, *small*, and *gift*. Making this effort will tighten up your speech and writing. It will also improve your grammar!

99. **Avoid false comparisons.** A false comparison happens when a person tries to compare two things but accidentally gets it wrong. Here is one example:

This year's race was faster than last year.

The writer is probably trying to compare this year's race with last year's race. Unfortunately, bad grammar has caused him or her to accidentally compare this year's race with last year, which makes no sense. It is a false comparison. The sentence could be corrected to read:

This year's race was faster than last year's.

Be careful to avoid false comparisons in your speech and writing.

100. Avoid ambiguity. Putting words in the wrong order can make your meaning unclear. Consider this example:

Dogs like digging holes and toys.

The writer clearly means that dogs like digging holes, but the way this sentence is constructed, it sounds like he or she is also saying that dogs like digging toys. This ambiguity could be cleared up by adding another verb so "toys" parallels "digging holes":

Dogs like digging holes and playing with toys.

Now the meaning of the sentence is crystal clear.

101. Pick your prepositions carefully. A simple preposition can change the entire meaning of a sentence. Therefore, you should always choose the best preposition to get your point across. Here is one example:

*Sean talked **during** dinner.*
*Sean talked **throughout** dinner.*

Can you see the difference in meaning? The first sentence implies that Sean talked sometime during the course of the meal. The second sentence implies that Sean chatted away the entire time. Both prepositions work, but the meanings of the sentences are quite different.

Here's another example:

*Barb tossed the ball **to** Rosa.*
*Barb tossed the ball **toward** Rosa.*

The first sentence implies that Rosa caught the ball. The second sentence, however, makes no such claim. We know that Barb tossed the ball, but the outcome of the toss is unclear.

Poor preposition choice can occasionally cause some funny mistakes. Here's an old favorite:

The port-a-potties were located in the trees.

This writer means to say that the toilets were located *beneath* the trees, not *in* them. It sure is funny to think of people having to climb trees to reach the restroom!

Don't let this type of mistake slip into your speech and writing. Paying attention to your prepositions will help you to say what you really mean every time.

Congratulations! You've completed this book, and you should feel more confident about your grammar skills. Now it's time to show off your newly acquired skills to your teachers, parents, and friends. Think before you speak and write to make sure you are using words correctly. You can always refer back to specific topics in this book if you are unsure about grammar usage in certain instances. Practice grammar rules and words that are troublesome for you, and soon you will be a great grammarian!

Answer Key

Chapter 2

Practice 1. Nouns in order of appearance: spacecraft, thud, forest, ship, minutes, door, side, ship, light, opening, doorway, figure, spacesuit, creature, bathroom

Practice 2. Pronouns in order of appearance: she, it, she, herself, it, her, she, it, she, he, he, she, his

Practice 3. Verbs in order of appearance: was, crawled, watched, pumped, tried, reach, played, shouted, ran, shot, beat

Practice 4.

1. Raoul tried to finish the <u>whole</u> burger, but he got (too) <u>full</u>.

2. The <u>fat</u> pig looked (amazingly) <u>cute</u> in the <u>pink</u> tutu.

3. Harriet (often) thought her coach was (quite) <u>funny</u>.

4. The parade was <u>long</u>, and it moved (awfully) (slowly).

5. The <u>slimy</u> worm (quickly) squirmed across the <u>wooden</u> table.

6. Jonah wanted to go (first) but the <u>new</u> kid beat him to it.

7. My <u>little</u> sister likes (only) (well) <u>scrambled</u> eggs.

8. The <u>best</u> <u>Halloween</u> parties have (very) <u>scary</u> pumpkins.

9. I am (fully) <u>aware</u> that the exam will be (extremely) <u>hard</u>.

10. <u>That</u> <u>ugly</u> <u>little</u> frog must leave (immediately).

Practice 5.

All possible answers are not listed here. You may have found other prepositions that worked.

1. on, upon   2. by   3. at, to, toward   4. before, during, in, throughout
5. from   6. on, with   7. before   8. across, under   9. around, behind,
throughout   10. after, during

Practice 6.

1. (Erin) (Deanna) and (Shereen) are best friends.

2. The little red (house) at the end of the lane looks deserted.

3. (Eggs) (flour) and a pinch of (salt) are needed for this recipe.

4. The (robber) thought the bank was open until 6:00.

5. The lazy (lion) slowly opened one eye.

6. While riding their bikes, the (boys) got caught in a storm.

7. (It's) raining cats and dogs.

8. The second (student) from the left just raised her hand.

9. The red (Honda) and the blue (Kia) raced down the street.

10. This filthy (floor) needs a good cleaning.

Practice 7.

1. Troy (couldn't decide) between the licorice and the mints.

2. The magic beanstalk (grew) and (grew) and (grew).

3. The green socks (would have been) a better choice.

4. Summer (came) and (went) in a flash.

5. We (gathered) tons of garbage at the clean-a-thon.

6. Maggie and Yvonne (talked) and (giggled) all night long.

7. Tarik (would like) to be elected class president.

8. That (isn't) my favorite type of music.

9. Georgie (could hear) her stomach growling during class.

10. My mom (will help) me to clean and cook the fish I caught.

Practice 8. 1. compound 2. complex 3. simple 4. compound-complex 5. complex 6. simple 7. compound-complex 8. compound 9. compound 10. simple 11. compound-complex 12. complex 13. simple 14. compound 15. complex 16. compound-complex 17. compound 18. complex 19. simple 20. compound-complex

Chapter 3

Practice 1. 1. like 2. like 3. such as 4. like 5. such as

Practice 2. 1. complete 2. run-on 3. fragment 4. fragment 5. complete 6. fragment 7. run-on 8. complete 9. run-on 10. complete

Chapter 4

Practice 1. 1. accept 2. except 3. except 4. accept

Practice 2. 1. affect 2. effect 3. affect 4. effect

Practice 3. 1. capital 2. capitol 3. capital 4. capital

Practice 4. 1. complement 2. compliment 3. complement
4. compliment

Practice 5. 1. stationary 2. stationery 3. stationary 4. stationery

Practice 6. 1. principal 2. principle 3. principle 4. principal

Practice 7. 1. than 2. than 3. then 4. then

Practice 8. 1. farther 2. further 3. farther 4. further

Practice 9. 1. lie 2. lay 3. lay 4. lie

Practice 10. 1. sit 2. set 3. sit 4. set

Practice 11. 1. its 2. it's 3. it's 4. its

Practice 12. 1. your 2. your 3. you're 3. you're

Practice 13. 1. they're, there 2. their 3. they're 4. there, their

Practice 14. 1. two, to 2. too, to 3. too 4. two

Chapter 5

Practice 1. 1. question mark 2. exclamation point 3. exclamation point 4. period 5. question mark 6. period 7. exclamation point 8. question mark 9. period 10. exclamation point

Practice 2. 1. semicolons in both spaces 2. colon 3. colon 4. semicolon 5. colon 6. colon 7. colon 8. semicolon

Practice 3. 1. It's 2. They're 3. didn't 4. Here's 5. wouldn't 6. weren't 7. We've 8. it'll 9. Who's 10. We're

Practice 4. 1. Robin's 2. leaves' 3. calves' 4. parrot's 5. Ed's 6. women's 7. oxen's 8. phone's 9. hamsters' 10. mice's

Chapter 6

Practice 1. 1. who 2. that 3. who 4. that 5. which 6. which 7. whom 8. who 9. whom 10. can 11. may 12. can 13. well 14. good 15. well 16. really 17. real 18. really 19. smell 20. stink 21. smell 22. less 23. fewer 24. fewer 25. *e.g.* 26. *i.e.* 27. *e.g.* 28. from 29. than 30. from 31. could 32. couldn't 33. couldn't

Chapter 7

Practice 1. 1. blew 2. snorts 3. had 4. ate 5. rolled 6. were 7. look 8. is 9. are 10. was 11. thinks 12. has been 13. its 14. costs 15. do 16. goes 17. scramble 18. meets 19. were 20. plays

Practice 2. 1. incorrect 2. incorrect 3. correct 4. incorrect 5. correct

Practice 3. 1. correct 2. dangler 3. dangler 4. correct 5. dangler

Practice 4. 1. incorrect 2. correct 3. incorrect 4. correct 5. incorrect

Bibliography

Azar, Betty Schrampfer. *Basic English Grammar, Volume A.* Upper Saddle River, NJ: Prentice Hall Regents, 1996.

Bartleby.com. *English Usage, Style & Composition.* Searchable database. Accessed April 2002. Internet. Available: http://www.bartleby.com/usage/

Johnson, Edward D. *The Handbook of Good English.* New York: Facts on File Publications, 1982.

Lederer, Richard, and Richard Dowis. *Sleeping Dogs Don't Lay: Practical Advice for the Grammatically Challenged.* New York: St. Martin's Griffin, 2001.

Pollock, Carroll Washington. *Communicate What You Mean.* Upper Saddle River, NJ: Prentice Hall Regents, 1997.

Index

Notes